AN ADVENTUROUS LIFE

Published in Australia in 2017 by
The Images Publishing Group Pty Ltd
ABN 89 059 734 431
6 Bastow Place, Mulgrave, Victoria 3170, Australia
Tel: +61 3 9561 5544 Fax: +61 3 9561 4860
books@imagespublishing.com
www.imagespublishing.com

Title: An Adventurous Life: Global Interiors by Tom Stringer / Tom Stringer, Marc Kristal.
ISBN: 9781864707335 (hardback)
Subjects: Stringer, Tom.
              Tom Stringer, Inc. (firm)
              Interior design firms—United States.
              Architectural design—21st century.
              Interior design.

Other creators/contributors: Kristal, Marc, author.
Maps (illustrations):   © Adriano Marcusso

Photography Credits
      Travel photography: © Tom Stringer
      Principal interiors photography: © Jorge Gera, with the exception of:
      Page 45: © Doug Snower
      Pages 88–90, 92 (left), 112–13: © Grey Crawford
      Pages 127–55: © Kristina Strobel
      Page 238 (upper right): © Werner Straube

Production manager | Group art director: Nicole Boehringer
Senior editor: Gina Tsarouhas
Graphic designer: Nicole Boehringer

Printed on 150gsm LumiSilk Art paper by Everbest Printing Investment Limited, in Hong Kong/China

IMAGES has included on its website a page for special notices in relation to this and our other
publications. Please visit www.imagespublishing.com

AN ADVENTUROUS LIFE

GLOBAL INTERIORS BY TOM STRINGER

Written with Marc Kristal

images
Publishing

CONTENTS

FOREWORD

I have known Tom Stringer for what seems like a lifetime. We both started our businesses years ago in Chicago, and Tom has been a terrific and loyal client—in our showrooms across the country, and in Chicago, where today he remains one of our top patrons.

Anyone who meets Tom will tell you that, in every way, he's what is commonly known as a great guy. He is generous, easy to work with, kind as well as smart, talented and creative, and possessed of great taste. Tom is also an excellent businessman. Tom Stringer Design Partners runs as effectively and efficiently as any studio that I've encountered. We at HH all love working with Tom and his team, and for his clients.

Even when you don't agree with Tom about something, he typically proves to be right in the end. And better yet, he is a happy man—and we both agree that happiness is as much a conscious choice as a natural condition. Very Buddhist, and very Tom.

Tom has a singular eye and appreciation for the unusual, an unorthodox spirit, and unbounded curiosity. Unwilling to take anything for granted, he travels the world to personally absorb cultures and bring back a variety of ideas and experiences for his work. What a great way to combine one's vocation and avocation and simultaneously build a great business!

The story here is not that of the more typical interior design book. Rather, it is a surprisingly forthcoming personal memoir, in part the saga of a life in design without boundaries, a life finding so much pleasure in discovering unusual beauty in unexpected places. A true world-class traveler, Tom never stops: he is a relentless seeker of the unknown, the exotic, the transformative and eternal.

This book is Tom's personal story at this point along his journey. I am certain that embedded in Tom's DNA is this empathic and generous curiosity about the wonderful, strange, and beautiful world that surrounds us, a curiosity that gives Tom's work its particular distinction. Quite simply, the man has gone places and seen parts of the world mort of us haven't. That global view is brought into every interior project that he creates.

An exceptional designer, Tom Stringer brings back to his work a balance of wit and sensibility, a vision joining consistency of home with a touch of the amazing "other" to his clients.

However, I do have a complaint about Tom. To date he has never invited me to join him on one of his fantastic voyages. But until then I am grateful to be able to journey vicariously through this many-splendored book—a trip I trust you will enjoy as well.

HOLLY HUNT

LOOMINGS

I have been an interior designer for roughly half my life—a fact that feels rather shocking, now that it's been set down on paper—and though I've written and spoken about my work on numerous occasions, creating this book represents my first opportunity to reflect, not so much on the reasons I do what I do (that's easy—it's all that ever truly interested me), but rather how I became the particular *kind* of practitioner that I am.

I'd like to say that the answer lies in childhood, and it does, in part. But my journey actually began long before I was born. It starts in 1893—in a town called Ashland, Ohio, with my great-grandfather, J.L. Clark. With his business partner, a Dr. Gilbert Hess, J.L. started a "farm remedies" firm called Hess & Clark. Though it may be hard to imagine from today's perspective that a great fortune could arise from hawking fly spray, udder ointment, and bird and cattle feed spiked with antibiotics, that is precisely what happened: my great-grandfather grew spectacularly wealthy, to the extent that he was able to fund Ashland's university and the town hospital before constructing his own mansion (an old-fashioned notion of "service first" that was instilled in me as a child).

Shortly thereafter, J.L. made a decision that has helped to define my life. Around 1904, he built a pair of cottages—one in the Queen Anne style, the other Arts and Crafts—on Mullet Lake in Michigan, just south of Mackinac Island. The largest nearby town, Harbor Springs, is where many of the name-brand Midwestern families, including the Fords, Wrigleys, Proctors, and Gambles, built their summer getaways and, indeed, Mullet Lake itself was colonized by a handful of turn-of-the-last-century industrialists whose relatives still come to visit. That's true of my clan as well. Today, my brother and sister and I share those cottages—there are 10 bedrooms between them, so there's plenty of room—and

though I've lived in many places, they remain my touchstone: all of us, and our extended families, still get together annually, and incredibly enough, our friends, there, are the descendants of the same people my great-grandfather got tipsy with over a century ago.

If that sounds insular, well, that was the point—and it has had a profound effect on my present-day profession. J.L. wanted us to be there *en famille*, rather than taking turns—that was never the idea—and as a result the cottages have become the repositories of my family's memories: that's where all the photos are kept, and the ancient home movies of Model T Fords motoring up and down the unpaved road in front of my great-grandfather's mansion. That generation, let me add, wasn't especially interested in fine art or objects. What they collected were moments of personal history—what the actor Jimmy Stewart famously called "pieces of time"—and the generations of my family have been strongly wedded to human experience, continuity, and connection, ever since.

As a designer whose work remains intimately braided with going places, I have always been attracted to one or another culture's talismanic objects, the things that draw meaning and potency from the stories attached to them. This interest, of course, derives from *my* talismans—those faded photographs and flickering reels of film—which relate my own family tale. As I have often said, to me, design is storytelling, and in fact I cannot imagine delivering an interior that, however aesthetically pristine, is devoid of personal narrative. My first, and perhaps most critical task, on every project, is helping my clients to distill and articulate their story: once I know it, we have a connection—one that gives direction, meaning, and resonance to the rooms that I create.

It was the next generation, specifically my maternal grandfather, that introduced me to what has become, not only a presiding influence on my work, but my life's great passion: travel. My grandfather, in fact, was a banker and an insurance man, and a quiet soul—he'd dropped out of college to help run the family business when his dad passed away unexpectedly, which I think gave him a certain reserve. And yet every Christmas he'd throw caution to the winds, and take the entire family on voyages that were on the one hand luxurious and on the other rather *outré*. In the late 1960s and early 70s, when the romance of commercial flight was at its zenith—747s occasionally had piano bars, and the stewardesses would slice prime rib on trolleys in the aisles—my grandfather decided, counter-intuitively, to revive the golden age of the railroad: he transported us all in a fleet of Cadillacs to Chicago's Union Station, and installed the family in a private train car, aboard which we journeyed to California.

This wasn't about showing off: rather, my grandfather believed it important for my generation to experience something that would soon be gone for good, a linear, land-based means of discovering America that was both high-style and surprisingly intimate. Nor were our frequent trips to Jamaica, where we were set up in villas that would have suited Ian Fleming or Noel Coward, devoted strictly to the sybaritic satisfactions of the Caribbean: my siblings and I, having learned to dive, attempted to make Jacques Cousteau–style underwater films, and sought out people in the community who introduced us to the island's unique cultural stew.

The idea of the informed adventure trip, where one goes someplace exotic and exciting that is also intellectually stimulating, was amplified by my mother, a modest but intrepid woman for whom a voyage down the Amazon, to cite an example, wasn't complete without an ornithologist specializing in the region's bird life along for the ride. That has become my own preferred mode of going places—one that has yielded, not only unforgettable experiences, but also a wealth of aesthetic, and human, information.

In the first chapter of *Moby-Dick*, "Loomings," the protagonist Ishmael describes the irresistible pull that bodies of water of every kind have on people everywhere—observing that what we see in them is nothing short of "the ungraspable phantom of life." So it is with me. Something that I have only recently come to understand is that the one constant in my life is water. As a boy, my father taught me to sail by taking me out onto a lake, diving off the boat, and swimming to shore, leaving me to figure things out on my own. Dad bailed on me—literally! But in so doing, he taught me to lose my fear, and become the master of my fate, lessons that have in every way stood me in excellent stead. Water links me to my childhood, moves me around the world (and to the sort of remote ports of call that would otherwise be unreachable), and—critically—offers a different way of *perceiving* the world. It is the common thread that pulls through everything I do: fueling my creativity, and freeing my soul.

WOODLAND TUDOR

Nothing in the world of interior design is inevitable. But it really does seem fated that the owners of this handsome Tudor house, on a 100-acre estate in Indianapolis, and I should have crossed creative paths. "We travel a lot, we know that you do the same, and we think that might be a good basis on which to build," they explained at our first meeting, a belief solidified by the discovery that my longtime love affair with Africa was more than matched by their own: the family created, and maintains, a wildlife preserve in Kenya.

How this might affect the renovation and redesign of a traditional Midwestern home became apparent when the couple showed me their extensive collection of African, and Afro-centric, objects and artworks—a collection awkwardly cohabitating with some fine Biedermeier pieces and furnishings in historic styles. The house, I felt, was divided against itself: my job was to edit, and bring focus to, both their African and European aesthetic and cultural interests, then integrate the two in a way that was comfortable and mutually enriching.

Before so doing, we cleansed the house's architectural palette, so to speak, by refining all of the interior moldings, hardware, and finishes, modernizing the kitchen and baths, and upgrading all of the systems. With this clean slate in place, we discovered that the traditional and vernacular, the historic and the exotic, fell naturally and easily into a mutual embrace. Working with my clients, I found them to be people of wide-ranging interests and tastes, some seemingly contradictory, all of which they brought elegantly into balance. I was gratified to see that the same proved true for the interior design of their home—a nest perfectly reflective of its singular inhabitants.

PREVIOUS PAGES: In the entry hall, an antique French commode, topped by an alabaster lamp, is paired with a contemporary cut-glass mirror; antique sepia-toned bird prints climb the stairwell. The dining room's hand-painted silk wallpaper contrasts with the fumed pine-paneled library. **OPPOSITE:** In the dining room, an antique Oushak carpet softens the limestone floor. **ABOVE:** A distinctive five-legged Georgian chair and French gilded bronze-and-mirror sconces grace the sitting area in the dining room's bay window.

PREVIOUS PAGES AND RIGHT: An overscaled painting by Todd Murphy continues the avian narrative begun in the entry, as the starting point for the living room. Biedermeier and French Empire pieces combine with a contemporary Asian lacquered coffee table. **FOLLOWING PAGES:** The family room mixes contemporary and traditional campaign furniture, both French and English, and features the clients' collection of artifacts brought back from Africa (where, in Kenya, they maintain a game preserve).

Previous pages: (Left) In the breakfast room, an African elephant sculpture and antique coin collection sit atop a contemporary sideboard. (Right) A framed mounted mudcloth, above a "wave form" bench designed by my office, in the back hall. **Above:** English bar stools and blown glass lanterns distinguish the kitchen island. **Opposite:** A curved banquette in the breakfast room's bay window.

Above and opposite: In the master suite, a photograph of a child from my clients' collection atop a reproduction English bedside table, and an intimate library nook with a rolling ladder.
Following pages: In a screen porch overlooking a lake, a table made from an antique Afghan door and Moroccan leather poufs mix with vintage-style wicker furniture.

CONTINUITY & CONSISTENCY

Working with a first-time client remains, for me, a keenly pleasurable experience, one akin to visiting a previously undiscovered country. In both cases exposure to a new sensibility compels me to look at design—and human nature—with fresh eyes. For all my wanderlust, I can be as prone to complacency as the next fellow. A new collaboration inevitably pushes me to challenge my assumptions, and invariably I, and my work, are the better for it.

And yet. I am a fortunate man in many ways, and perhaps most of all for having the privilege to design multiple homes for certain individuals and families, in some cases across several decades. Shaking up one's creative sensibility, embracing the shock of the new, provides a fresh perspective. But working with repeat clients is immeasurably enriching in other ways: it enables me to revisit, explore, and expand upon ideas that may require years to fully gestate; to develop a richer understanding of the individuals for whom I am designing, and to bring that more nuanced knowledge back to the drafting table; to be educated by old friends even as I do the same for them. As there's no better way to get to know people, in my view, than to travel with them, having longstanding relations with a client enables both of us to observe one another's responses to new experiences, so that, over time, we can alert each other about things to see, places to go, artists or craftspeople whose sensibilities might enrich our own. Long-time clients are my collaborators, my patrons, my confessors, my muses. Without the continuity and consistency that they bring to my life, truly, I could not do what I do.

Something else I have observed about the people for whom I work repeatedly: they tend to treat their interiors with the same sort of care and consideration that they give their artworks, antiques, and collectibles. The great interior designer Albert Hadley recalled that his partner, the legendary Sister Parish, was only disheartened by her clients when they didn't maintain their homes and freshen them up periodically with a coat of paint or new upholstery. I understand: while interiors (with certain exceptions) are not meant to last forever, they are nonetheless products of the imagination, habitable stories written by commingling the visions of a designer and his or her clients, with contributions by a raft of artisans of every sort. I wouldn't compare my office to Parish-Hadley. But I take great pride in what we do, and am fortunate to have clients who see value in—and take pleasure from—treating our rooms like living works of art.

One of the most interesting aspects of an interior design project, paradoxically, is its connection to the exterior world beyond the windows and walls. This is particularly the case with a house, of course, where site, landscape, architecture, and decoration all exist in relation to one another. But it can be equally true of an apartment, where an attractive view becomes, in effect, a part of the daily living experience.

Many of the people I've worked with more than once are well aware of this, and not a few have responded by acquiring the properties that surround their original homes, and requesting that I help knit them into a cohesive experience. The impulse typically derives from another kind of continuity: the desire to make room for subsequent generations, places to which children, and grandchildren, will look forward to visiting. The value of a longstanding professional relationship becomes especially evident when this happens: after traveling with my clients, after diving or climbing or ballooning with them, visiting galleries and museums, or even just gazing at a water view over a glass of wine, I've absorbed—actually and instinctively—a great deal about what they value in terms of family, legacy, and what it is that really matters. So when I extend the borders of their properties, I'm enlarging, not just their living experiences, but their lives—and doing so with a privileged, intimate knowledge.

As I have often said, no one needs what I do. But within the purview of my profession, I can bring people joy, for today and a long time to come. As Cole Porter might have put it: That ain't hay.

AT HOME IN THE CITY

I've written at length about my global circumnavigations.
The Chicago house I share with my husband, Scott, represents a
circumnavigation of life: its location, a block from Lake Michigan,
is a short distance from our first apartment on Lake Shore Drive.
And though the distance between the two addresses is negligible,
the road Scott and I have traveled together has been complex,
circuitous, and wonderfully enriching—all of which is amply
reflected in our home.

The 19th-century structure, with a projecting two-story addition
appended in the 1930s, combines a Norman roofline with a Beaux-
Arts façade, to appealingly eccentric effect. We chose it, in part,
for its defiance of the city's grid. In Chicago alleyways serve as the
principal means of ingress and egress, and we didn't want to come
and go from the back all the time. Our house has a driveway, and
occupies a lot that's extra wide and extra deep—which means that,
not only can we enter from the street, there's enough room for both
a garden and a garage.

Our tastes are somewhat at odds—if it's neoclassical, modernist,
or ethnographic, I'm all in, whereas Scott appreciates a dose
of Victoriana. Yet we've managed to bridge the gap both
architecturally and decoratively. Regarding the former, we strove
to create a unified, English-influenced neoclassical interior. The
decorative synthesis derives from the fairly exotic collections
that grew out of our far-flung travels, which nest naturally and
comfortably within the more traditionally elaborated rooms.

I'd be highly critical of someone who decorated a residence while
wondering "what does this say about me?"—yet I was forced to
ask myself that same question. As in all matters, however, a strong
partner is a good foil. And as our journey came full circle, I found
that everything that is best about who we are, individually and as a
couple, came to the fore, to produce a home that is warm, centering,
and sure to last.

adam and steve   kelli snively

PREVIOUS PAGES: Our house's exterior mixed Beaux-Arts and Norman influences. In the foyer, a contemporary giltwood-and-mercury glass chandelier hangs above a chevron-patterned white oak floor; a German Deco console is flanked by Russian Regency chairs upholstered in Fortuny fabric. A Cole Sternberg mixed media piece hangs beside a rosewood Steinway piano in the living room, which also mixes antique and contemporary French and Asian furniture with Polynesian shell money, scrimshaw boar tusks, and Oceanic "give-back" figures, all collected on our travels. RIGHT: In the silver-leafed dining room, two sets of 18th-century French dining chairs, square- and round-backed, are matched with a mahogany dining table. A Burmese headdress made from yak teeth, which we found at Inle Lake in Myanmar, stands atop a vintage Karl Springer console table, paired with two African fertility figures.

OPPOSITE: A gilded mirror hangs above a chest finished in steer-horn marquetry, and reflects a Yoruban beaded crown and Oceanic shell currency. ABOVE: African bronze fertility figures above the Karl Springer console.

LEFT AND FOLLOWING PAGES: The generously scaled barstools at the kitchen island can be turned to face the adjoining "keeping room," which features an antique farm table that's been cut down to serve a different purpose. Above the sofa, a contemporary Aboriginal "water" painting that Scott and I acquired on a visit to Uluru.

RIGHT AND FOLLOWING PAGES: In the master suite, with its silk wall covering, hangs the antique French chandelier Scott and I acquired for our first home. The walnut burl armoire is the very first antique I purchased, as a college sophomore, with a $300 birthday check from my grandmother. In the sitting area, I placed a French marble-topped guéridon adorned with a Songye culture African mask; the gilded Empire table in the corner features a repeating Sphinx motif. The white marble bath sustains the suite's subdued color palette.

ABOVE, OPPOSITE AND PREVIOUS PAGES: The quiet character of the library is reinforced
by the men's suiting flannel covering the walls. On the marble mantel, a Surrealist painting
Scott and I discovered in Italy is flanked by tattoo pens found in Myanmar and an African
mask. My office designed the tufted leather ottoman. An antique English "tilt-top" table
and Louis XVI–style chairs, ideal for backgammon and cards, stand before the bookshelves.

RIGHT: One of the three third-floor guests suites. The 18th-century neoclassical French chair is upholstered in a Fortuny fabric; the large Satsuma vase Scott inherited from his father. Two works from Robert Longo's "Men in the Cities" series hang above the settee.

AT SEA

Once I felt comfortable enough, as a boy, to sail on my own, the world opened up to me in unexpected ways. There was, of course, the opportunity—tantalizing, to a 10-year-old—of independence. It's hard to imagine nowadays, in a world of helicopter parenting, but for me, Mullet Lake was a place where you got out of bed in the morning, disappeared for the day, and no one gave it a thought if you didn't return until dinner. Accordingly, I'd climb into our little Whaler, a kind of single-masted rowboat that could accommodate one sail, undertake the 4-mile crossing of the lake, and pass the hours exploring an uninhabited beach before heading home as the sun set. It was, for a child, tantamount to circumnavigating the globe; and to this day, the prospect of setting my own course, unencumbered by expectation or, in particular, the need to find shelter upon arrival, is one of life's keenest, most dependable pleasures.

That early experience also revealed to me two things that proved highly relevant to my profession. The first was the idea of the self-contained, movable house, which is how I've always seen even the smallest of boats. My interest in living in motion no doubt began in the aforementioned private rail car, a beautifully designed and fitted-out, fully equipped residence that could also carry you, in style, across the continent. Eventually that evolved into an interest in Winnebagos: I used to beg my grandmother, when we went on outings together, to take me to RV sale lots, so that I could study the many variations of mobile home on display, and marvel at the efficiency with which they were designed, constructed, and kitted out.

Ultimately I realized that I had a fascination with systems, which became an underpinning of my design work decades before I actually became a designer. I began drawing the plans and elevations of houses, on graph paper, in the third grade, and a transformative moment for me was coming across a Toro sprinkler-system catalogue in a hardware store. My mind grasped the concept immediately, and as a result the next house I drew included a self-sustaining landscape (one that was also fully illuminated, thanks to my next discovery, a Malibu lighting-system brochure).

Boats, trains, mobile homes, of course, are all examples of carefully worked out, fully integrated systems, all of them functioning seamlessly and simultaneously to produce an effect, and that has become one of the hallmarks of my work—an ability that has served me especially well in the design of ocean-going yachts. Something I also learned, as a boy designer, about systems: you can never be aware that they exist, as if you are, it's generally because something's stopped working. The perfect correlative is the human body. We walk, talk, sleep, eat, breathe, think, laugh, create, fall in love, and never give a moment's thought to the extraordinary collection of internal systems that make it all possible—unless one or another ailment interrupts the flow. That's what I strive to create as a designer: serene, elegant interiors that respond at every level to the needs and desires of my clients—and never, ever catch cold.

I should add that my father's preferred method of sailing instruction—jumping overboard and leaving me to fend for myself—also stood me in good stead when, as a design student at Arizona State, I unexpectedly found myself running a business. In my freshman year, I was hired by the decorating firm Kitchell-Newlon as a part-time, all-purpose assistant, and quickly got promoted to associate designer. Both Nancy Kitchell and Brad Newlon were wonderful to me, at that complex moment when I was coming of age, coming out of the closet, and coming into my own as a professional. Nancy taught me about eclecticism, showed me the power of opposites, and celebrated individuality; Brad taught me how to be a man, demonstrated the value of honesty and self-respect, and generously mentored my emerging design sensibility. It is impossible for me to overstate my debt to them, or my affection and gratitude.

THE Sometime STORE
SO NA GA   ENA SITOA

Brad also showed me the kind of confidence-building trust that every aspiring creator should receive. In my second year with the firm, he departed to open his own studio, and took me with him. Shortly thereafter, Brad developed health problems requiring an extended leave of absence—and simply handed me the reins. As things transpired, he was absent for a year, necessitating that I drop out of school; but after Brad came back, and I started taking classes again, I had the kind of practical experience that made me, in effect, a peer to my professors. That enabled me to absorb what they had to teach in a more comprehensive way than if I'd had no hands-on knowledge whatsoever.

I don't know that I'd recommend it to everyone. But I find that I learn best by being compelled to fend for myself. It makes one imaginative, resourceful, and—especially useful in the design world—cool under pressure.

As noted, I began diving when our brother recruited my sister and me as kids, to help him become the next Jacques Cousteau. (The housing for the underwater movie camera, alas, proved so unwieldy that we were defeated.) After that, it was decades before I next strapped on a scuba tank, and then it started, really, as a lark: Scott and I took a resort diving course on a cruise. But after that, having become certified, we were able to make an open-water dive in the Caribbean, and Scott, who'd never tried it before, found it to be an entirely exhilarating experience. His enthusiasm reconnected me to the pleasure I'd known as a "camera assistant" in the waters off Jamaica, and we resolved to dive again as soon as an opportunity presented itself.

I have always, whenever possible, sought to travel with my design clients: there is no better way to get to know someone, and to absorb one another's tastes, preferences, and styles of living. It was on just such a trip, to the Bahamas, that the true satisfactions of diving were revealed to me. Without telling us, this particular client invited Scott and me on what turned out to be a shark dive, in the course of which you observe—intimately—the

hand-feeding of a school of sharks. We were, of course, petrified, but wimping out wasn't an option, and so we eased ourselves into what we assumed would be troubled waters. The experience proved to be transformative. To be surrounded, literally, by 50-odd sharks, bumping you as they glide past, is to discover what beautiful, indeed lyrical, creatures these beasts of legend can be. Rather than scaring us half to death, the dive proved to be surprisingly energizing—and launched us on an ongoing journey, to discover the world's least explored, most far-flung destinations: places we'd otherwise never visit, peopled by cultures we'd never have gotten to know.

One of our early voyages introduced us to the Tuamotus, an archipelago of islands and atolls some 500 miles north of French Polynesia, and one of the most remote destinations on the planet. We sailed into a deep lagoon, surrounded by a fringing reef of sand and palm trees, beyond which lay the roiling waters of the South Pacific. Though the lagoon was utterly becalmed, a break in the reef allowed the current to flow in and out with the changing tides—bringing with it a vast school of sharks on the hunt for sustenance. Dropping down some 40 feet, we looked up through shafts of refracted sunlight and observed as these sacred monsters undulated through the waters above us. Seldom have I felt so intensely alive.

It's not all about dancing with sharks, of course. What you don't realize about scuba diving until you become proficient is that it's the closest thing to flight that an earthbound mortal can experience. When you're diving in currents—drift diving, as it's called—you slip into the water in one place knowing that you're going to be taken to another, and the experience is tantamount to being a bird riding the winds. Your breathing and your movements are controlled, to minimize expenditure of air and avoid spooking the abundant sea creatures, and so you learn how to rise or fall simply by inhaling or exhaling—becoming one with the water in which you're immersed.

SOCIETY ISLANDS, LEEWARD

Maupiti

Bora Bora

Taha'

Raiatea

Huahine

TUAMOTU ARCHIPELAGO

Tikehau

Rangiroa

Raitahiti

Toau

Fakarava

Tahanea

PACIFIC
OCEAN

SOCIETY ISLANDS, WINDWARD

Mo'orea

Tahiti

Polynesia

And—*and*—what you're flying over is terrain that doesn't exist on land: peaks and valleys of the most unimaginable beauty and exoticism. As a designer, I am, of course, endlessly fascinated by the surfeits of color, pattern, texture that saturate the sea; I've expended entire tanks of air trying to snap a single photo of a fast-flowing anemone, the beauty of which I want to bring back home. And there's so much to explore—caves, reefs, outcroppings. It is not too much to say that I emerge from a dive in a state of ecstasy, my mind and soul steeped in the sea's sublimity.

You can image that the chance to expand my design palette would be irresistible—but no less so is the opportunity to discover the most unfamiliar societies. Though it's perhaps obvious, one of the most extraordinary facts about traveling aboard a private yacht is that you can go places that remain otherwise entirely unreachable; places where commercial air or sea travel is not only next to impossible, but unimaginable. On a dive trip that Scott and I took with friends to Fiji, we found ourselves approaching an island that hadn't received an "outside" visitor for over a year. Upon arrival, we observed a ritual: after granting permission to disembark, the island's chieftain invited us to a greeting ceremony called a *sevusevu*, which involved bringing an offering of kava root, a traditional expression of respect; from this is made a fearsome-looking brew that, when drunk, produces a mildly hallucinogenic effect that remains central to the ritual's exchange of pleasantries. Once we were all accepted, the community welcomed us with dance and music, a social embrace the likes of which none of us had ever experienced. I love to dive, and the visual extravaganza it presents is in every way threaded through what I do. But it is this communal aspect of travel—the chance to believe, for a moment, that we are truly all sisters and brothers—which I've come to value most deeply.

The acquisition of objects, moreover, enables us to bring that communal spirit home, and has come to inform the way I collect. Many of the places we've visited have art and craft works that are unique and indigenous, be they carvings, scrimshaw, pottery, textiles, or even larger and more elaborate pieces. The things I choose are beautiful and unusual, of course, but essential to what makes them interesting is a connection to place—both the experience of a particular locale, and my feelings about the artisans and makers who've introduced me to their work. As I have said, for me, design is storytelling, and whether I'm collecting for my own home or advising a client on a purchase, I don't believe in decoration divorced from meaning. Whatever goes into a home—a *true* home—should be a component of the residents' personal narrative: something that adds nuance and texture to the saga of a well-lived life.

I realize that traveling on dive boats to exotic lands may seem exclusively to be the purview of the privileged. But our journeys have always been in pursuit of adventure, aesthetic and cultural enrichment and, not least, individual enlightenment. And the objects we've collected are neither trophies nor souvenirs, but rather talismans—with all of the resonance of the sepia-toned photos that reside at Mullet Lake.

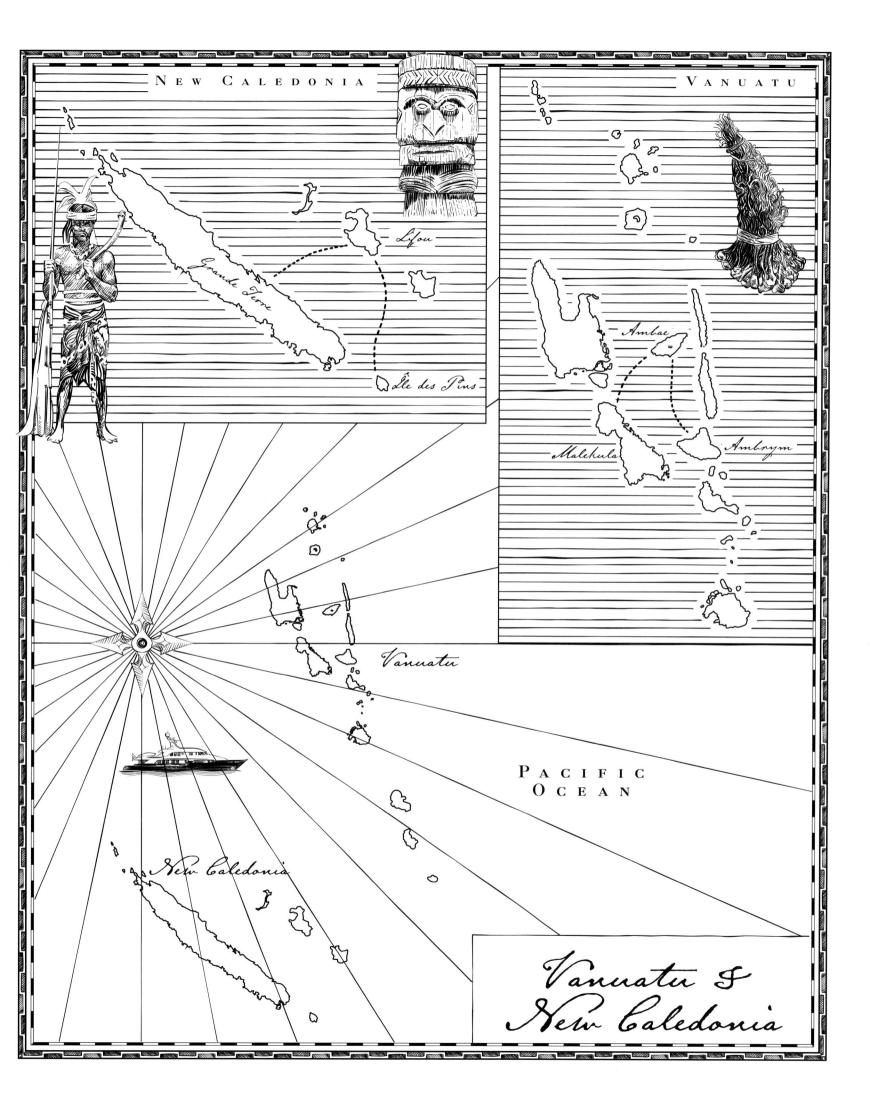

NEW CALEDONIA

VANUATU

Lifou

Grande Terre

Île des Pins

Ambae

Malekula

Ambrym

Vanuatu

PACIFIC
OCEAN

New Caledonia

Vanuatu &
New Caledonia

COASTAL RETREAT

This Santa Barbara estate, which commands a low bluff above the Pacific coastline, absorbed nearly eight years from commencement through completion—and benefitted extensively from the knowledge I gained from season to season.

The residents are people who enjoy both the satisfactions of nest-building and far-flung travel equally. As such, California's central coast was an excellent place to put down roots: it is at once specific and timeless, possessed of a strong sense of place, but also an evanescent character that suggests a multitude of environments. The fact that there was room for a rambling structure proved fortuitous, as this home was meant to be one that multiple generations could enjoy together: it's always been my observation that togetherness works best when there are places to which one can escape.

We wanted the structure to reflect the relaxed character of a classic California ranch house, with a low-slung roof, dormers, board-and-batten construction, and an architectural open-endedness suggestive of a place that had been added onto over time. By contrast, I was aware that this very laid-back beach house would contain a sophisticated art and photography collection, as well as fine furniture and objects. Within that dichotomy—the vernacular and the refined holding one another in a pleasurable tension—lay the key to vitalizing the interiors.

As almost everything for the house would be newly acquired, my clients and I decided that we would create a collection from scratch at the beginning of the design process, one that would help establish the residence's particular character. This we accomplished by acquiring, at a stroke, a selection of multicolored Anglo-Indian lanterns, nearly 30 in total. We hung them in one of the pool pavilions, where their elegance, exoticism and cheerfulness caught the overall mood to perfection: every time you turn the lights on, it feels like a party—no need at all for balloons.

OPPOSITE AND PREVIOUS PAGES: The pool cabana combines the board-and-batten walls and exposed beams of the California ranch style with teak cabinetry and a custom teak pool table, handcrafted surfboards, and a collection of antique Anglo-Indian lanterns my clients and I discovered in New York.
ABOVE: A pair of massive bronze wall fountains by Albert Guibara anchor the entry courtyard.

The reclaimed teak pool pavilion was hand-built in Bali to render its character distinct from the house's California millwork. An antique Laotian rain drum and a contemporary lacquered Chinese sideboard encourage an air of exoticism.

RIGHT: In the long hallway off the living room, a canvas by Joan Mitchell, one of a handful of blue-chip artworks made all the more arresting by the casual beachfront context. **FOLLOWING PAGES:** A painting by Cecily Brown presides over the mix of antique and reproduction furnishings in the living room (there is a second fireplace at the room's opposite end). The relaxed elegance of the upholstered pieces contrasts appealingly with the vernacular architecture.

OPPOSITE AND ABOVE: A collection of pottery by Axel Salto layers the view from the living room to the formal dining area across the hall, where a painting by James Rosenquist commands the eye. A contemporary gilded chandelier hangs above a 17th-century French dining table.

ABOVE AND OPPOSITE: A cross-axial connection from the dining room through the hall to the living room unites the front garden with the back lawn and ocean view, and encourages a sense of light, space, and openness—California living at its most relaxed and refined.

ABOVE AND OPPOSITE: The kitchen, which overlooks the casual sitting area just past the house's front door, is finished in a pale walnut. We used a sliced mosaic green serpentine stone for the countertops and backsplash.

ABOVE AND OPPOSITE: The kitchen communicates with a casual dining bay, distinguished by nearly full-height sash windows offering a 180-degree view of the Pacific. The antique French iron chandelier features rusted—and rustic—tole.

LEFT AND FOLLOWING PAGES: The warm, wood-paneled library, which communicates with one end of the living room, incorporates objects and collections from a range of periods and cultures. On view are Tibetan hats, African figures and boxes, a Robert Graham bronze atop a vintage Jacques Adnet table covered in vellum, and Dutch Deco tub chairs.

RIGHT AND OVERLEAF: In the second-floor master suite, which overlooks the water, an antique Syrian mother-of-pearl chest, at the foot of the bed, conceals the TV.

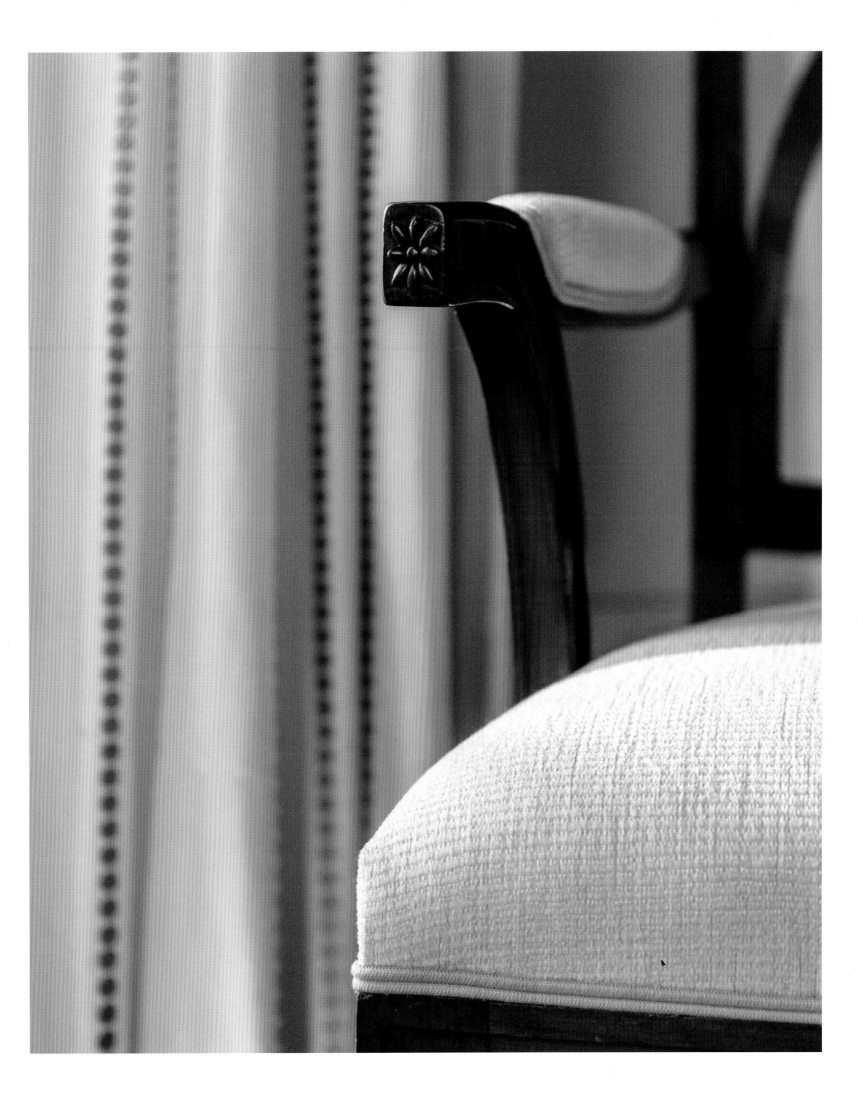

ABOVE: An Alsatian carved pine console, Spanish gessoed candlestick lamps and Regency-style mirror grace the entry to the master suite. **OPPOSITE:** A pair of distinctive polychrome wooden doors, which the residents discovered on a trip to Turkey, forms the portal to the guest wing, which features a series of elegantly cut Moroccan lanterns.

In a guest suite, an antique Anglo-Indian four-poster bed rests atop a contemporary Turkish rug. The large abstract canvas is by Judith Dolnick, and was originally acquired by the seminal California decorator Michael Taylor for a client in 1970.

The guest sitting room features gessoed mirrors and a chandelier, all from Argentina.
In a house filled with treasures of every sort and stripe, two of my favorites can be
found here: a pair of elephant footstools from the late, great Barnum & Bailey Circus.

CARTOGRAPHY & AUTHENTICITY

As you have seen, many of my travels are out of the ordinary, and the objects and artifacts I discover on those sojourns can be startling in their singularity. Just as many of my trips bring me to destinations that are broadly familiar, as are the pictures and furnishings I encounter in these places. Yet no matter where I find myself on the map, I'm always in search of things possessed of a trifecta of qualities: they must be authentic to the place; they must be a genuine reflection of that place; and, not least, the particular character of their authenticity must be appropriate to the new place in which I plan to install them.

How can something be specific to a particular location and not express its character? Let me offer a food analogy. You can find extraordinary sushi in Rome—but how, really, are the two connected? They may coexist, but that doesn't make the sushi "Roman". The same thinking applies to the objects I introduce into an interior. They are there to amplify the larger story of the design scheme, or to add what might be described as a subplot—but if they aren't real, and an honest expression of their origins, the story those objects tell will be the wrong one, or even misleading. They may "look" alright. But they'll spoil the sincerity of the rooms in which they reside and, consequently, those spaces will never feel entirely comfortable.

The challenge of authenticity is complicated by the oft-stated but nonetheless essential fact that, with the rise of the global village, it becomes ever harder to find things that are, in fact, what they appear to be. That makes the real things that much more important, for the simple reason that they matter more. So when I do find an object that arises from and reflects an indigenous tradition—whether in Texas or Tahiti—I cherish it and make sure the piece finds its way into the appropriate situation.

In a beach house my office created on California's central coast there are two interesting examples of the confluence of authenticity and cartography—one that was found, and another that we made. The former involves a beautifully crafted doorway my client discovered in the far east (and purchased with my blessing) that we used as a portal to the beach house's guest wing. Because local building codes prohibited us from constructing a freestanding structure, the guest accommodations had to be connected; yet we still wanted them to feel singular and special. Accordingly, the wing is reached via a fully glazed architectural "hyphen" that bridges a small stream—at the end of which we set the exotic polychrome doorway, the introduction to a new experience both domestic and decorative. I could have hung a solid-core door there, it would have served its purpose adequately. But by bringing in an unusual craft object—one that signified, in its original locale, the portal to adventure—my clients' houseguests feel as though they're going on a journey.

I confess that the second element, the one we developed, gives me a special satisfaction. It's an open-air pool pavilion that, to give the part of the garden it occupies a distinct, slightly magical character, different from everything else on the 5-acre property, we had crafted from my design in Indonesia. In execution this proved to be quite complicated, for we had to make the structure's stainless steel welded frame in southern California (in order to comply with local seismic codes). Once that was completed, the frame was shipped to Indonesia, where the fabricators slip-fitted it into the teak outerstructure, then dismantled the thing and shipped it back.

Yes: we could have had the pavilion built by the same talented California woodworker who crafted the kitchen cabinets and other elements. But then it would have felt like the rest of the house—the structure wouldn't have had the frisson that derives from being authentic. Now it is an Indonesian pool pavilion, rather than a California building done in the Indonesian style. And that makes all the difference.

THE YACHT SLOJO

The first purpose-built yacht designed by my office, in collaboration with the boatbuilding firm Delta Marine, *Slojo* conflates two ideas, one having to do with treasure hunting, the other with the satisfactions of home. My clients, global nomads and ardent collectors, have been gathering objects from the world's most exotic ports-of-call, and displaying them in their homes, for decades. With *Slojo*, they are able to travel, collect, and showcase simultaneously, aboard a movable residence that reflects its own ongoing journey.

It sounds lavish, but the 156-foot-long boat is in fact rather modest, a reflection of its primary function as a vehicle for scuba diving. *Slojo* has, of course, been crafted to the most exacting specifications, its straightforward purposes supported by complex and elaborate systems. But that was a good part of the fun: my clients and I spent a lot of time chartering comparable yachts of every sort, and analyzing their layouts and amenities. We "sea tested" many of our ideas before putting them into practice.

For the interiors, we rejected the European-influenced minimalism then dominating the yachting world, preferring a softer, more enduring approach. As my clients and I were traveling together extensively in Africa during the design ideation process, the patterning found in the continent's textiles found its way into the carpets, curtains, and veneers. Because *Slojo* was meant to be a family boat, the spaces themselves were tailored to be more intimate—we put our focus on the rituals connected to the joys of friendship, and absorbing the worlds above and below the surface of the sea.

Slojo was a project that both benefitted from my experience with yachts and contributed to it. I am most grateful for what was an entirely unique design opportunity—and, thanks to the considerable generosity of my clients, the chance to enjoy the outcome as well.

PREVIOUS PAGES: The lower aft deck features a comfortable, easily rearranged suite of teak furniture. The marble-topped pedestal table, custom crafted for the boat, is anchored to the deck but can be moved to take advantage of the path of the sun. LEFT, ABOVE AND OVERLEAF: The main salon's custom-designed woven carpets, curtains, and upholstery abstract motifs from traditional African textiles. A pair of Tang Dynasty terra-cotta earth spirits guard the entrance to the salon. The bookshelves feature highlights from the owners' ever-evolving collection of African and Oceanic objects. The distinctive cocktail table is lacquered faux tortoise.

In the dining room, just off the main salon, Jean-Michel Frank–inspired chairs surround a contemporary table. The antique Tibetan painted chests flanking the portal between the rooms were restored and retrofitted for silver storage.

OPPOSITE: The dining room's Tibetan painted chests were discovered on a shopping trip my clients and I made to Hong Kong. ABOVE: The stairwells feature anigre paneling, stainless steel railings, and custom carpets, all designed by my studio. A cornucopia of objects found while exploring, including one of a pair of 8th-century terra-cotta earth spirits and a warrior's shield from New Guinea.

PREVIOUS PAGES: In the master suite, an African-inspired carpet hand-woven in silk, a collection of antique calligraphy brushes on stands, and a contemporary lacquered zebrawood stool serving as a cocktail table. **RIGHT:** A pair of butterfly-matched onyx slabs distinguishes the master shower. The dressing table holds a small collection of antique jewelry and a Tibetan arm cuff.

PREVIOUS PAGES: In the semi-circular entry to the four guest suites, the sole object
is an Oceanic warrior's shield. Anigre millwork complements the limestone floor.
LEFT: The elegance of the guest suite belies its functionality: the mirrors conceal a
large-screen TV and storage space hides behind walls upholstered in woven horsehair.
Beside the bed (ABOVE) a silver relief depicts the deity Vishnu.

PREVIOUS PAGES, ABOVE AND RIGHT: *SLOJO*'s Sky Lounge is finished in Mozambique veneers set off by nickel fillets. The silver-mounted candlesticks are made from polished kudu horns collected in Africa, and the two antique oil paintings—rare finds—depict Pompeii's destruction by night. FOLLOWING PAGES: My office designed the chaises and the torchères, which serve as a repeating motif on deck.

WHY YACHTS MATTER

Allow me to offer an observation that, though it seems convoluted, is entirely accurate: what is extraordinary about a yacht is that it's a machine masquerading as a house—though at heart, it is really a hotel. So: what might that mean, and how is it relevant to the design of landlocked interiors?

Essential to the idea of a luxury yacht is "yacht service," which by nature and necessity has to be on a par with what you'd expect in the world's very finest hotels—that is, service that anticipates your needs to an almost telepathic degree. In part, yacht service involves things like the appearance of a gin-and-tonic at your elbow just as the thought enters your mind that you might like to have one. But more important is the kind of elaborate ballet that has to go on to make living in what is ultimately (and no matter the square footage) a confined series of spaces feel natural and, in particular, seamless. For example, let's say you leave your stateroom in the morning to go to breakfast, then return half an hour later to find the bed made and everything immaculate. How does the steward get in and out of your cabin without being seen in a passageway carrying a vacuum cleaner and fresh linens? The answer is that concealed in your space behind a false wall is a closet containing all of the necessary maintenance and provisioning materials—and every suite on board is comparably outfitted.

That represents, of course, an extraordinary level of service. But it's also an extraordinary design opportunity, one that I have found to be at once exhilarating and overwhelming. There is the simple fact that, on an ocean-going yacht that may spend three months away from its homeport, everything that you might need for that journey (other than fresh produce) has to be stowed, seaworthy, and stable.

The calculations are endless, ranging from how much rice or flour needs to be onboard (and where does it go, and how does it remain fresh) to how many sets of flatware and china will be required to keep your guests consistently enchanted at mealtimes. When you're not under sail, how do you avoid subjecting the people on board to the vibration and noise (and odor) of the engines? On a yacht that I designed (as always, in conjunction with a master boat-builder), all of the interior architecture floated on rubber cushions—and everything within those cushioned rooms was cushioned as well.

For a systems-loving individual like myself, yacht design is Nirvana: there are systems involving service, maintenance, security, preservation, and much, much more—and they all have to be at once fully integrated with one another, and individually accessible and discrete. For this reason—and although, relative to the total cost of the machine, the interior design budget is comparatively austere—the level of craft far exceeds what is generally available for land-based projects. Indeed, only firms specializing in yacht construction can produce the millwork and furniture. A case in point: I specified zebra wood paneling for a boat lounge that featured a nickel fillet as a design motif. On land, we'd simply insert four pieces of wood into a joint. For the boat project, however, these four pieces had to be dovetailed, then secured with machine screws—and that was *one component*. When you consider that a mega-yacht is a 10,000-square-foot house offering white-glove service that can also take you anywhere in the world and ride out a hurricane without so much as a glass breaking, what you're really talking about is crafting the equivalent of highly refined timepieces that are 150 feet long and four stories high.

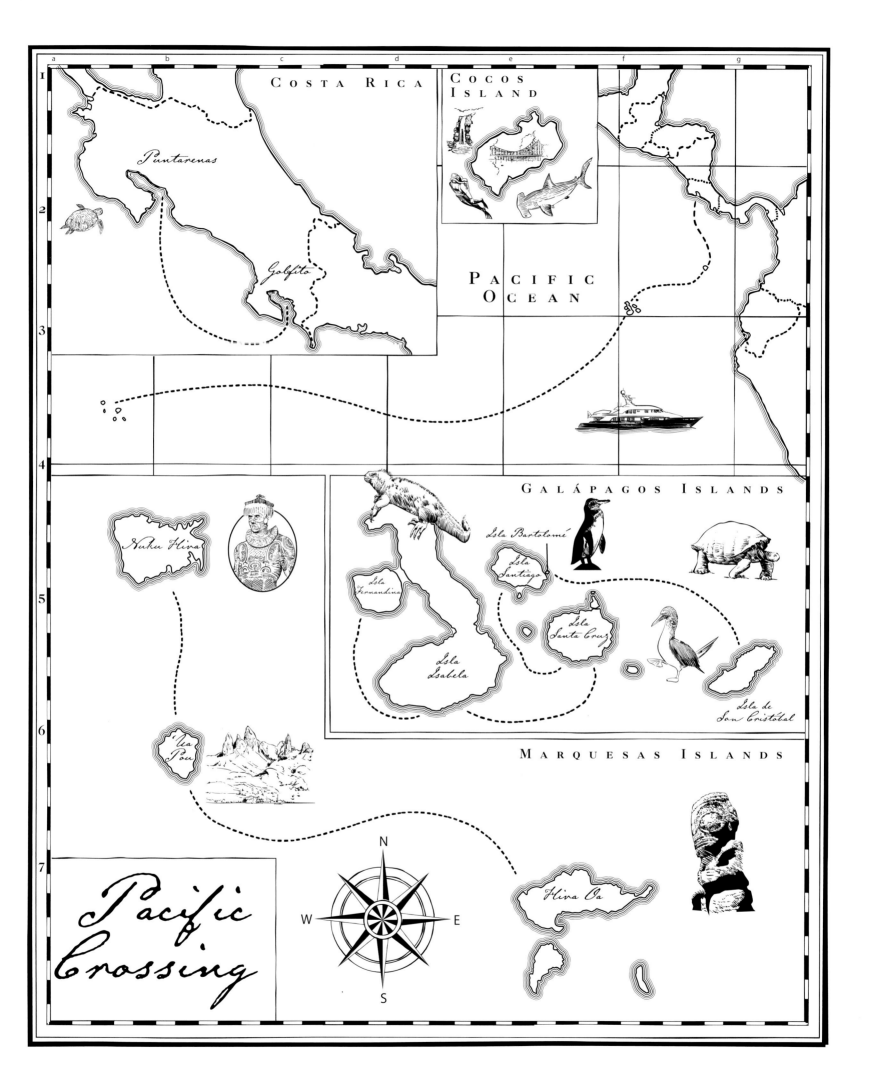

a　　　　b　　　　c　　　　d　　　　e　　　　f　　　　g

1

COSTA RICA

COCOS ISLAND

2

Puntarenas

Golfito

PACIFIC OCEAN

3

4

GALÁPAGOS ISLANDS

Nuku Hiva

Isla Bartolomé

Isla Santiago

Isla Fernandina

Isla Santa Cruz

Isla Isabela

5

Isla de San Cristóbal

'Ua Pou

6

MARQUESAS ISLANDS

7

Pacific Crossing

N

W　　　E

S

Hiva Oa

In my experience, and no matter your profession, meeting highly specific challenges has a positive impact on the totality of one's capacities, and this has proven to be very much the case with my work on yachts. Increasingly, I find myself creating homes for clients with complicated programs requiring considerable back-of-house support. And making them not only beautiful, pleasurable places to inhabit, but exceptionally high-functioning, consumes more and more of my creative imagination.

This can be as simple as ensuring that a staff of six can service a house without making their presence obtrusive—or as complex as making a multi-million-dollar project feel as artless and casual as a seaside cottage. Indeed, for one such "beach shack," I faced two challenges that were especially daunting. The first involved developing an HVAC system that would enable my clients to throw open their doors to the sea air and fluctuating climate without causing environmental damage to their world-class art collection. The other had to do, oddly enough, with noise abatement: though the residence overlooked the Pacific Ocean, and the soothing ebb

and flow of the surf remained clearly audible, it was also close enough to a major highway to be periodically plagued by traffic noise. The solution: a series of discreetly positioned outdoor microphones that captured the waves breaking on the beach and water features on the property, and piped them into the house via concealed speakers—sounds that were amplified automatically during rush hours, and modulated once the traffic abated.

As a devotee of Chicago's rich theater culture, I know how easily the mesmerizing spell of a sublime stage effect can be dispelled by an offstage crash or the unintentional appearance of a stagehand. Similarly, I love nothing more than to commission craftspeople to execute my bespoke furniture designs, travel the world in search of beautiful and usual decorative objects, to select just the right upholstery, or to advise a client on the purchase of a painting. But I know that even the most arresting interior design can be undermined if I don't devote equal time to the crafting of what goes unseen. I pride myself on having the skill to do so—and I have the brain-twisting challenge of yacht design to thank.

LAKESIDE GUEST HOUSE

I often describe a yacht as a machine that masquerades as a home while also being a hotel and a restaurant. This project, which sits on the shore of a lake in Grand Rapids, might accurately be described as a landlocked yacht.

In fact, it is actually a stand-alone extension of a house, designed very specifically for entertaining. My clients welcome guests frequently, and often on a grand scale, for both business and pleasure, and remain discerning connoisseurs of haute cuisine and fine vintages. Accordingly, they wanted an at-home version of a private club, so as to be able to host people in a genuinely gracious way.

As yachting enthusiasts, they were aware of the high level of accommodation that can be achieved in a compressed space—*if* the right infrastructure has been put in place. With that in mind, they allowed us to apply the principles of yacht service, to create a pavilion that is warm and residential in character, but also contains within it a second layer of extreme functionality.

The style duplicates that of the main house, in essence a somewhat streamlined version of Prairie. Yet that is perhaps the only aspect of the building that remains fixed. The great room can be arranged to host dinners for a dozen, or the lounge furniture removed to welcome banquets of 50 or more; a high-speed freight elevator facilitates the movement of furnishings between floors. The elevator also enables connection between the custom-designed demonstration kitchen adjoining the great room, and the industrial-grade set-up on the level below. The bar is the equal of what you'd find in the most elegant of settings, and two guest suites complete the program.

You can't hoist the sails, it's true. But as would be the case on a well-designed vessel, most needs have been thoroughly anticipated—and everything required to fulfill them remains perfectly in place.

PREVIOUS PAGE, LEFT, ABOVE, AND OVERLEAF: The Great Room, with its rustic stone fireplace, hand-sawn walnut floors, and Australian cypress ceiling, replicates the "contemporary Prairie" style of the main house. The furniture can be removed via a high-speed freight elevator and the room reconfigured to accommodate dining for up to 60 people. Bronze-finished chain mail curtains separate the space from the adjoining kitchen. The oil and metal leaf painting is by Cynthia Rutherford.

Previous pages: The bar features backlit onyx panels, hand-blown glass light fixtures, and ceiling panels upholstered in top-stitched leather. Two four-top tables (inspired by Giacometti) complement the quartet of bar stools. **Above and opposite:** Refrigerated steel-and-glass wine cases separate the custom-designed and crafted stainless steel kitchen from the bar. A door at the room's far end opens onto a high-speed elevator connecting to a more robust service kitchen and scullery on the floor below.

174

Previous pages, above, opposite, and overleaf: The guest suites
feature silk carpeting, woven horsehair for the walls, and hand-embroidered
linens. Among the surprising details: a coffee table by the artist Jim Zivic,
crafted from a lump of anthracite coal.

QUALITY & DICHOTOMY

If I were compelled to choose two, and only two, aspects of my nature that most inform my design approach, I believe I'd select my attraction to opposites and, especially, my inclination to go to extremes.

Regarding the latter, I suppose it was instilled in me by my parents, via that tiresome yet essential nostrum, "Anything worth doing is worth doing well." I resented hearing that as a kid, but they're the words I live by today. To a fault: I carry my extremes to extremes. Once I decided I loved scuba diving, to cite an example, I plunged in (so to speak), and by now have experienced it over 500 times. There's no point in pursuing excellence or experience if you're not willing to take it to the limit, and I apply that conviction to matters both personal and professional.

Extremism is, of course, a cousin to my attraction to opposites, and also tightly intertwined with it. I am equally inspired by the highly mechanized and richly organic, the finest of the fine contrasted with the elemental and quotidian. And my office is relentless about combining them in ways that seem artless, unlabored, and inevitable.

Fortunately, I'm someone who is inspired, rather than daunted, by complexity. Most of our projects are supported by copious amounts of interdependent technologies, and my office explores them fully—there's never a moment when we say, "Enough already!" That is because design development really is like peeling an onion: there's another layer, then another, and each reveals ever more fascinating detail.

Interestingly, the methodologies for creating the perfect technological support system, and finding the ideal craft object, furnishing or painting, are quite similar: both require a systematic approach. People have often remarked on the uniqueness and diversity of the things I discover on my travels—but each trip is meticulously planned, and structured to bring me into contact with the most unusual objects of desire. Similarly, if I'm assembling a portfolio of art and antiques for a client, finding those objects requires research, documentation, and relationship-building, a system for the pursuit of beauty, if you will. In the old days, it was perhaps more challenging: you'd have to get on the phone to dealers and collectors around the world and explain what you had in mind, and then receive a packet of Polaroids in the post three weeks later. Today, I can search global aesthetic databases online; input the dimensions, components, species of wood, and the style, and get back the top five available choices in minutes; click a mouse, and in a matter of days, the precise thing that I'm looking for shows up at the office via air freight. But now as then, creating an artful, elegant interior that feels as though it just naturally came together requires an exceptional amount of rigor.

I am fortunate to have clients who share my passion for pursuing perfection. What I've always found interesting is that, despite their differences—some are committed and diligent art collectors, others superlative musicians who've spent decades hunting down rare recordings and scores—they are united by an obsession with quality. The challenge for me is to link each individual's passion to a comparable excitement about design, to make a connection that becomes a way in. Indeed, one of the essential weapons in my professional arsenal is the ability to develop an enthusiasm for what I do in others. If you've read this far, you know that I love my work, and I flatter myself that I'm good at it—but never forget that, enfin, nobody really needs a big, multilayered interior design project. Thus I spent a lot of time creating desire in my clients—the desire to engage with the process imaginatively, enthusiastically, and at the very highest level.

True, there's a bit of obsessive compulsion to it—after all, I'm a guy who can't leave my own house without styling it for my return. But there's also a profoundly satisfying pleasure to be found in the work, whether I'm piecing together a sprawling underground "situation room" that will drive every aspect of a residence, or creating a cradle in a drawer for a salad fork. As someone who appreciates the theatre, I am always aware that behind a seamlessly executed production, there are a myriad of components, each of which required an infinity of patience and meticulousness, and multiple decisions, to get just right. So it is with what I do—and the satisfaction I feel when a homeowner beholds the outcome is every bit as sweet.

VENICE BEACH VILLA

It doesn't require a philosopher's wisdom to know that the voyage of life takes as many unexpected twists as travels that traverse the globe. This house, a short walk from the Pacific in the oceanside community of Venice, California, fully expresses that truism: it served as a bridge back to unity—personal *and* aesthetic—for a formerly married couple that chose to reclaim their relationship.

The structure itself was the ideal setting for a renewal of intimacy. The house's H-shaped plan, with its wings overlooking serene interior gardens, forms an oasis of privacy and peace. The place had been designed by an architecture writer with a discerning eye for detail, and the overall experience developed with considerable care and forethought. Best of all, the residence afforded the opportunity for husband and wife to install many of the objects they'd collected—both separately and together—in previous lives, and create a base for going forward anew.

In fact, the pair's core collection had been developed, by them and myself, for several residences of theirs that I'd designed previously—in a sense, the objects were reunited in much the same way as the owners. I took a keen pleasure in knitting these components back together again—in remembering the lives they'd lived previously, and renewing their artful acquaintanceship in unexpected ways, even as I kept the overall design scheme simple and casual: appropriate for the beach setting, and a good foil for the rigors of the architecture.

As a designer, I seek to create a sense of layered history, even in projects that remain the equivalent of a new penny. In this house, I was afforded the rare opportunity to do the opposite: to shape a fresh perspective out of things resurrected from a complicated past—and in so doing, to make a path to the future.

PREVIOUS PAGES: The entry incorporates a 1970s brass console, a hair-on-hide upholstered bench, and a chandelier made from glass and rope. The L-shaped living/dining room opens into an enclosed inner court shaded by magnolias. ABOVE: A granary door executed in wood and bronze. OPPOSITE: A vintage Jens Risom walnut, lacquer and travertine console, topped by African artifacts, including a trio of walking sticks.

RIGHT: For a corner of the living room, we refashioned a massive carved Thai teak panel into retractable doors that conceal a large movie screen. **OVERLEAF:** The dining room features a contemporary lacquer table from Thailand, large oil painting by Mariangeles Soto-Diaz and an ancient Chinese bust-shaped inspiration stone.

RIGHT AND ABOVE: The keeping room, which adjoins the kitchen, includes Danish Midcentury dining chairs upholstered in raspberry linen, a contemporary Aboriginal painting from Uluru, and a bust adorned with beads and skulls.

OPPOSITE AND ABOVE: The breakfast area, off the kitchen at the foot of the main stair, incorporates cerused oak, stained concrete floors, and stainless steel countertops. OVERLEAF: The upstairs hallway, with the master suite at one end and a library and two guest suites at the other, overlooks the courtyard. Atop the built-in console: Tibetan singing bowls and an African mask. The early Danish modernist cabinet at the hall's far end is constructed from raffia, walnut, and bronze.

LEFT: In the master bath, a pedestal, Baga culture bird head, and Deco-inspired hand-woven rug. A contemporary table is fashioned from an antique Indian marble elephant; the trio of hanging lanterns are Persian. **OVERLEAF:** The master bath mixes a bronze four-poster, a mounted Yoruba beaded crown, and a photograph by Paco Peregrin.

A MINOR IN ASIA

One of the most overused, and frequently abused, descriptive words in the world of design is "Asian"—it has come to mean everything and nothing. To some decorators, an Asian interior suggests a judiciously curated selection of antiques, fabrics, and finishes derived from extensive research and thoughtful consideration. To others, it means a trip to a furniture showroom. Given this state of affairs, I have a very hard time conceiving of Asian design—or, for that matter, Asia itself—as a single, undifferentiated entity.

And yet. My travels thus far have been relatively limited—Scott and I have visited Hong Kong and other parts of China, Singapore, Myanmar, and Thailand—but an introductory dip into these diverse cultures has given me a larger understanding of Asian art and design. What I have observed, across the board, is that the artisans of the East aren't intimidated by layering or complexity, or the prospect of taking a long time to create a single, small thing. That doesn't mean that the arts of Asia are complicated, fussy, or difficult to appreciate—quite the contrary. Rather, it reflects a belief that simplicity isn't the only way to arrive at a positive outcome—a good lesson, in my view, to take home to the West.

My initial visit to China began in Beijing, and followed a fairly typical tourist trajectory through museums and cultural attractions, as that's really the only way to see what is left of historic China. We took in the Great Wall, an experience of deep emotional resonance; saw the mausoleum of Qin Shi Huang, unified China's first emperor, which is protected by an extraordinary army of some 8000 terra-cotta soldiers; and spent a day at a "panda research center," where we were able to play with two young bears, an event so magical that it bordered on the surreal. Finally, we departed via Shanghai, a city, once known as the Paris of the East, that interleaves history and modernity, Eastern and Western influences, in ways that are highly seductive. Zipping around from district to district on motor scooters, we did very little in the way of collecting: much of what we saw was the product of commercialization, and there is a difference between something made in China and "Made in China."

Subsequent visits enabled us to slip beneath the surface of the obvious, one of the most memorable being the trip to Myanmar, in part because it felt so mystical, so separate from the modern world. The most singular destination proved to be Inle Lake, in the north, where we encountered a floating society that's been farming on the water for eight centuries, a place akin to a primitive Venice. No one, interestingly, could satisfactorily explain how this came to pass. Scott and I speculated that the story might have been similar to that of the community on Lake Titicaca in Peru, where the culture shifted from land to water to escape its enemies; alternatively, as Inle is surrounded by exceptionally steep mountains, the waterborne society might have evolved from necessity, as there was virtually no farmable land.

Whatever the case, Inle Lake struck me as a singular demonstration of opportunistic design: of how the most creative solutions often derive from nothing more or less than a response to existing conditions. We passed days observing the handcrafted bogs on which life is lived; the balletic grace of the fisherman as they cast their nets, balancing on one leg while simultaneously paddling their boats with the other; the incongruity of the high-tension wires strung from bamboo poles (heaven help the electricians there); and the elegance and serenity of the families of weavers.

From there, we journeyed to the ancient city of Bagan (once called Pagan) in the Mandalay region; we went ballooning at dawn above the vast plain of temples, monasteries, pagodas, and stupas, constructed between the 11th and 13th centuries, that are the city's signature. North of Cambodia, due east of India, the architecture (once we began our earthbound investigations) proved to be a beguiling mélange of styles, combining South and Southeast Asian influences.

I also did a fair amount of collecting in Myanmar. A quarter to a third of almost every interior that my office creates is bespoke, in part to shape a given project for a client, but also because it is often easier to design and build what I see in my head than to find it in the marketplace; I often say that my designs are externally inspired and internally driven. Yet there is a special pleasure to be had from particularizing a room with craft, if the objects you find are unusual, appropriate to the residents and the overall design intention, and have interesting stories behind them. In Myanmar, my great discovery was a garage-style workshop that produced exceptionally lightweight water-gilded lacquerware. Watching the makers craft a piece, I was struck by the delicacy of the woven reeds used to construct the form. The resulting object is at once surprisingly sturdy and pleasingly refined: precisely the sort of contradiction with which to accent a space.

Myanmar also raised an interesting question in my mind, one that derives from the difference between Inle Lake and Bagan. At Inle, people created a community where there wasn't one—really, where there shouldn't even be one—and produced something rich, complicated, beautiful, and unique. Whereas at Bagan, the indigenous community was extracted: all the people were removed to preserve the monuments as a kind of architectural/cultural museum, which is fascinating and important, but deprived of everyday human context. The contrast spoke, to me, to one of the central challenges of design. How do you create an interior that functions at multiple levels, in which the aesthetic grows out of and supports that functionality? And how do you introduce beautiful objects into a home without turning it into a museum—and thereby combine beauty with the vitality of everyday life?

As is evident, that single trip set my mind moving in multiple directions. But that, to me, is the amazing thing about travel: it seems like no matter where you go, or how many times you go there, you've only just scratched the surface. I've been to that part of the world perhaps 10 times now, but if you asked me if I were a major Asian traveler, I'd have to admit that I am still an Asia minor. And there's no knowing how many times I'll have to return before I feel like what used to be called an "old China hand"—which suits me just fine.

Southeast Asia

MYANMAR

LAOS

Bagan

Inle Lake

Chiang Mai

BAY OF BENGAL

Yangon

THAILAND

ANDAMAN ISLANDS

Narcondam Island

Bangkok

Smith Island

Outram Island

Barren Island

Havelock Island

ANDAMAN SEA

South Andaman

LINCOLN PARK PENTHOUSE

The enduring American mantra "there's no place like home" is especially applicable to the dynamic metropolis that is my hometown. And I have seen few better places from which to behold Chicago than this Lincoln Park penthouse. The wraparound terraces embrace the entirety of the park, a layered water view, and the iconic vitality of Michigan Avenue. I looked forward to the lively challenge of creating interiors the equal of that special Chicago magic.

This was to be my office's second residence for these clients, very avid collectors with highly specific tastes. When we first met, their interests were in all things English, and my task involved relaxing their home, so that the bounty of their Anglophilia could be more readily appreciated. By contrast, the new penthouse was a tabula rasa, for which I was to create a new collection—one that would engage the owners' enthusiasm in a way that might compel them to continue it.

We began with French neoclassical furniture and a selection of objects I'd characterize as a "Franglish" mix—French, English, and Chinese—all of which infused the home with a patina of worldliness. From there, I explored ethnographic art, and eventually found a path to early 20th-century modernist paintings, many with a Chicago connection, which linked the time- and space-traveling interiors to home—and set my clients' collecting passions aflame anew.

I'm happy to say that what began with my influences has now been completely taken over by my clients' energies—my office may have supplied the dynamite, but they lit the fuse. Well-traveled, curious people with an eye for quality, they're adding to and curating their collections avidly. That spirit of renewal is everything I could wish for a home.

PREVIOUS PAGES, LEFT AND ABOVE: The apartment's linear hallway is interrupted by an ellipse—decorated with a Biedermeier table, Asian ceramics, and an African sand-cast bronze "tree of life"— which opens onto the living room. The grand space, with conversation-stopping views of Lake Michigan, Lincoln Park, and the Gold Coast, draws together 18th-century painted French fauteuils, a clean-lined sofa, and tub chairs of my own design. Chinese ancestors gaze down from the wall while a pair of Tang dynasty horses rest on the glass-topped cocktail table.

PREVIOUS PAGES: (LEFT) In the living room, a klismos chair by T.H. Robsjohn-Gibbings stands before an English giltwood-and-lacquer secretary. (RIGHT) At one end of the dining room, I combined a modernist canvas in oils, an Ekonda culture chief's hat, and a marble-topped mahogany French Directoire demilune commode. **ABOVE:** A three-armed wall sconce from the famed French design atelier Bagues. **OPPOSITE:** A 17th-century bronze chandelier hangs above a Regency-style dining table of my own design.

Previous pages: Bar stools surround a quartz-topped kitchen island. Cabinetry lightly separates the space from the family room. A large oil by Albert Krehbiel lends a sunny note. **Above:** White quartz covers the kitchen countertops. **Opposite:** A Poul Henningsen pendant light above a Saarinen table in the breakfast room.

LEFT: In the master bedroom, an antique Swedish neoclassical painted commode. The small oil painting is by R. Leroy Turner. **ABOVE:** The master bath.

A rich Prussian blue glaze envelops the library. Atop the contemporary hand-woven rug, a John Saladino side chair and a bronze-and-zebrawood cocktail table. An Edwardian lantern, composed from faux bamboo gilt bronze, and green glass, hangs above a painting by Frances Chapin.

ORIGINALITY & SPECIFICITY

I am going to begin with a slightly heretical observation. To wit: Originality is overrated. Let me explain.

Many decorators will say that the perfect client is someone who lets them design everything in a residence—the furnishings, the fabrics, the case goods, lighting, tableware, you name it. Certainly I've fantasized about a job like that, in which every last component was original to me. And then I think: How boring! The poor client would feel as though he or she were living in a Tom Stringer–designed jail (luxurious and well-run, of course, but nevertheless). In fact, such titans as Mies van der Rohe and Frank Lloyd Wright practised this kind of soup-to-nuts design and realized it brilliantly. Yet even they became experiential micro-managers of the homes they created. While I am a self-confessed extremist—ironically, the one thing I don't carry to an extreme is the need to be original.

In fact, I come from the opposite point of view, which is that the elements one picks up along the road to a finished project, whether by accident or design, are precisely what add vitality and originality to a home. They can be iconoclastic and robust, like the tables the artisan Jim Zivic hews from chunks of coal. Or they can be playful, for instance the "elephant footstools" from Barnum & Bailey's Circus that we set in a family's sitting room, where they serve the same purpose (though for much daintier feet).

Such "finds" also bind people more firmly to their homes as, in addition to enriching the decorative story, they also provide people with stories to tell. Indeed, my office has often been asked to provide clients with "information sheets" regarding the elements in one or another room, so that they're more accurately able to convey what it is that makes them unusual or interesting. In addition to increasing a family's pride in a home, the pleasure to be had from being, in effect, one's own docent also inspires the impulse to learn more, and collect more (and with greater erudition). I could do it all, and perhaps some day I'll try. But those eccentricities, even in the most restrained, well-mannered room, are absolutely critical.

Of course, that doesn't mean I'm averse to bespoke creation. The pattern my office typically follows is to collect the components of a house's story, then custom-craft the pieces necessary to enable them

all to connect in a meaningful way. I was unable to find the right log set for the living room fireplace in one of my projects—I just wasn't seeing anything that suited the particular character of the room—and so I approached a sculptor, who responded to my charge by finding old merlot and chardonnay vines and casting them in bronze: a highly original, elegant solution that was as distinctive, as right, as anything we might have discovered.

Whether found, or made, every aspect of all of my projects is carefully considered and, consequently, highly specific. This has the opposite effect of making a house feel over-managed or too tightly controlled: being certain that each element of a residential experience has been taken into consideration frees the people inhabiting it to relax and enjoy the ride. For a client whose level of meticulousness was equal to my own (to cite one example), I designed the recessed lighting ceiling plan so that not a single light trim intruded upon the seam between two boards—a mind-bending exercise for a 12,000-square-foot residence, but one that never fails to bring satisfaction to the sensibilities of the owner.

That last point is key. To execute that lighting program, I had to find a builder who shared my and my client's obsession with detail, and our passion to get it right no matter what it took. A builder whose attitude amounted to "eh, it's close enough" would have failed, even if I'd stood over him with a horsewhip. Similarly, I would never impose my own obsessions on a homeowner to whom they didn't matter—if I did, my client would feel mugged, not enriched. Rather, I and my colleagues spend time getting to know the people for whom we work, paying close attention to their likes and dislikes, then pursue the particular kind of perfection that has meaning to them.

Just as originality for its own sake can amount to showing off, it is important to be specific about what one needs to be specific about, a lesson I learned from designing yachts (an endeavor in which, if you let a detail slide, it will do so quite literally). I try never to forget that a home is about the people who live in it, and not a designer's ego.

GOLD COAST WATERSIDE

When I travel, the objective is typically the pursuit of the undiscovered. This southern Florida residence, however, grew out of a voyage to a land I'd visited multiple times, at the specific request of my clients—and quite adroitly answered a very particular set of challenges.

The project began when I suggested to this couple that they purchase a waterside house that was under construction— it had great bones, a full program of inviting spaces, high ceilings, and, alas, all the wrong details. When I assured my clients that the problems could be corrected, they accepted my suggestion, we edited the plans, and a developer's special began its transformation into Architecture.

While the building was being completed, these people—knowing of my affection for the city—asked me to show them Marrakech. The way in which I'd characterized its exoticism had piqued the pair's curiosity, and they wanted to see the place through my eyes. And though we didn't go specifically for inspiration, their observation of how Moroccan architecture engages with a hot climate and a searing sun—mitigating the light, shaping cool courtyard spaces—led them to request that we try similar gambits in Florida.

Upon our return, I set about investing the house with a distinctly North African sensibility. Within and without, we paved the project with highly polished white limestone. The front and rear gardens were walled to create courtyards. Interior spaces, too, we treated like enclosed courts: the soaring, sometimes double-height rooms received *mashrabiya*-like screens to soften the tropical sun while casting elegant, ever-shifting patterns on the walls and floors. The outcome is at once very Miami and very Moorish, a contemporary expression of a timeless, supremely elegant style.

PREVIOUS PAGES: In the entry foyer and stair hall, white limestone and glass meet a two-story dark-stained teak wall screen inspired by my trip with the owners to Morocco. We had the screens fabricated to our design in Bali; the bronze and black glass table is by Holly Hunt. In the great room, I designed the rug based on a pattern seen in Marrakech, where I also found the mother-of-pearl inlaid tea table; the chair riffs amusingly on the zebra photos and pillows. A photograph by Michael Noonan presides over a dining table, joined by a pair of zebrawood benches. LEFT: A trio of repurposed African spider tables above the kitchen island. ABOVE: Chocolate lacquer and white limestone in the breakfast room.

251

ABOVE AND OPPOSITE: The game room is dominated by a well-stocked bar with a quartz top and antique mirror sides. The bookshelves were designed by my studio. **OVERLEAF:** The study, paneled in gray-stained rift-sawn walnut, features rolling screens that replicate the pattern seen initially in the stair hall. The collection of photographs dates from the 1960s and 1970s and includes iconic images from photographers Harry Benson and Sylvie Blum.

RIGHT: The screens appear again in the austere, elegant dining room, where a trio of photographs by Sean Gallagher keeps company with a Cambodian teak statue. The klismos form dining chairs are some of my favorites from Michael Taylor.

ABOVE AND OPPOSITE: The stair ascends to a second-floor lobby, where we set
a mahogany and stainless steel early French modernist table found at auction.

ABOVE AND OPPOSITE: Grillwork cabinets made in Bali and lined with melon-colored silk
brighten the master bedroom. I love the crazy chair, which I found through a Florida antique
dealer—I think of it as a Moorish riff on a rector's chair, for a fabulous Palm Beach priest.

Right: The grillwork pattern turns up in the master bath's rolling screens. Beyond them, a covered terrace for massage treatments. The photograph is by Paco Peregrin. **Overleaf:** A sitting room in one of each of the two guest suites features and oil and wax abstract by Lynn Basa and a series of mixed media self portraits by Flora Borsi.

INTO AFRICA

As with Asia, there is no such thing as "African" design because there isn't one Africa. Every nation on the continent—in fact, virtually every region—has its own artistic, cultural, and craft traditions, ranging from the entirely indigenous to the completely imported (though more typically a blend of the two, stemming from a palette of Colonial and contemporary influences). Within its borders, to a degree that has surprised and astonished me for half my life, lies all the world.

As it happens, one of my earliest interests as a designer had to do with African ethnographic art. In my early 20s, I came across a pair ceremonial drum-beaters from Chad in a gallery in, of all places, Los Angeles. I found them both transfixing and affordable (the collector's holy grail), and these objects formed one of my first purchases, quickly followed by others, thanks to the stateside prevalence and availability of ethnographic pieces. But what I also discovered was that African tribal art comprised one component of my attraction to juxtaposing the raw and the refined. One of my earliest gambits—both for myself, and my clients—involved pairing African and French neoclassical pieces. Opposites, I believe, amplify each other; and in my first starter condominium, a nest of industrial chic with catwalks and pipe rails, I incorporated Gallic antiques and tribal artifacts—it was an experiment and, believe me, it was the bomb.

When I began traveling on a regular basis to Africa, some two decades ago, and started to acquire objects at their source rather than from dealers, I discovered another dimension to my interest, one that ran deeper: what drew me to ethnographic art proved to be its utility—however intriguing or beautiful those objects might have been, they also served a purpose, usually social, religious, or ceremonial. That understanding was an early, crucial contributor to my perception of design as *storytelling*.

Let me add that a large measure of Africa's exoticism, at least to me, derives from its diversity. My initial visit there, in my very early 20s, was with my mother, and for sheer drama it has proven hard to beat. There we were, Mom and I, on camelback in a desert near the Algerian border, in the company of the Tuareg, a nomadic tribe famed for their blue skin (the result of the indigo dye that leaches out of their garments). A sandstorm delayed us for a day, and the Tuareg welcomed us warmly into their community, giving me, among other gifts, my first taste of pigeon pie, a thin-crusted delicacy sweetened with sugar. I will tell you: eating pigeon pie with blue men in a desert sandstorm is the acme of cool—and to top it all off, it was Mother's Day.

Morocco revealed to me so many things, perhaps uppermost among them the arresting character of Islamic architecture, which proliferates in parts of North Africa. To be exposed to the Islamic style, with its sublime, hypnotic mix of regional forms and the timeless principles of Western classicism, is to have your notions of beauty forever changed.

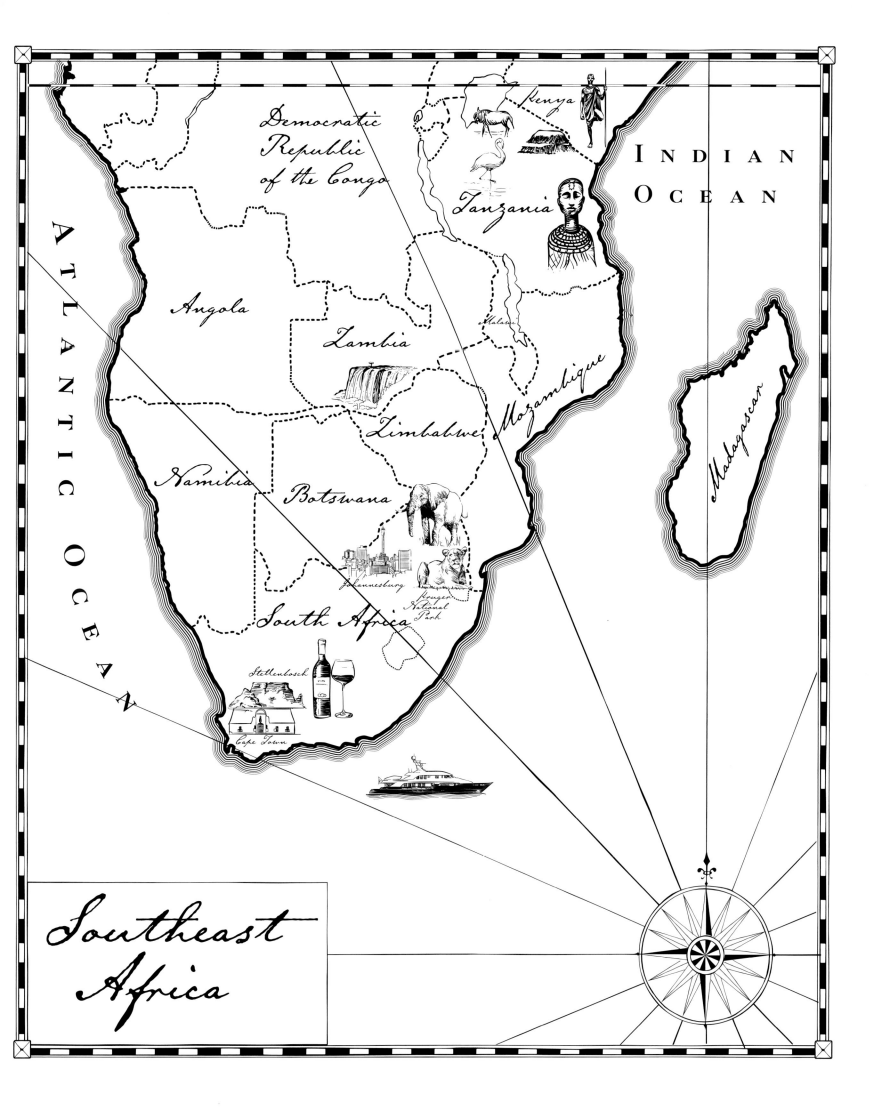

If there is variety on the African continent, Morocco offers variety within variety. The 12-acre Jardin Majorelle in Marrakech, designed and developed in the 1920s and 30s by the artist Jacques Majorelle (the radioactive cobalt blue he used throughout still bears his name), later purchased by Yves-Saint Laurent, represents the French Colonial influence at its most sublime. The city of Fez stimulates me for a very different reason: a walk through the souq, with its rattling ox carts and gutters running red with the blood of slaughtered animals, the austerity and cacophony, thrust one back into the 8th century, an experience I find enlivening and energizing. The whitewashed plaster structures that characterize the seaside city of Essaouira suit the temperate climate and way of life. And the architecture of the high Atlas Mountains is the most unexpected of all: in some villages, crenellated castles of mud and stone, and in others alpine-style chalets that would not be out of places in Gstaad. With apologies to Hemingway: it is Morocco that is the true movable feast.

Egypt, of course, is also a part of Africa, and when Scott and I journeyed down the Nile from Cairo to Aswan a few years ago, on a well-appointed *felucca* (the traditional Egyptian sailboat)—a voyage that seemed to draw us back inexorably to the origins of civilization—it was the realization of a lifelong dream. We visited the great temples of legend, and explored the contents of several burial sites not ordinarily open to the public (I know: *Tom Stringer, Tomb Raider*). But what might be called my "working eye" was most strikingly engaged by the ancient art of surface decoration, in particular the subtleties of the very shallow bas reliefs executed in stone. The lucid Egyptian light brings out the intricacies of these planar designs exceptionally: the subtleties of the lines and how they define shapes, barely revealed yet remarkably descriptive. When we returned, I began to incorporate that planar delicacy into the molding profiles of the interior architecture within certain projects, moving our designs away from the more typically pronounced Western aesthetic.

You never quite know where you're going to find inspiration, or how inspiration will find its way into your style. But of this I'm sure: some of our clients would be surprised to learn that the subtly gradated door frames and crown moldings in their homes derive from the Pharaonic reliefs decorating the great temples of ancient Egypt. Such are the great gifts of travel.

GOING THE DISTANCE

Some fifteen years ago, my husband Scott and I made a choice that has reshaped our lives—and my work—in transformative ways: we decided that three to four months each year would be devoted to exploring different parts of the world, places that are either entirely unknown to us, or old geographical friends that have yet to yield all their wonders.

Various factors influenced this decision. The most significant were personal: my mother and Scott's dad were both diagnosed with serious illnesses, and almost precisely at retirement age, when they assumed they'd at last have the leisure to do as they wished. That taught a powerful lesson. It had always been my expectation that Scott and I would work hard, close up shop, and hit the road, and the realization that this plan could be torpedoed by the caprices of health (or the depredations of old age) made us think that we'd best chase our dreams while we were still nimble enough to catch them. Exploring the world is what lets me do what I do: Travel enables me to enrich and renew the wellspring of my creativity, explore a multitude of aesthetic possibilities and, critically, to understand the cultures that gave birth to them. I cannot overstress the importance of this idea: an object, no matter how beautiful or unusual, is just an object—if my awareness of its origins and meaning do not underpin the reasons I've chosen to bring it into someone's home. Thus it remains essential, not only that I continue to discover new things, but understand the context from which they emerge.

Another reason was that, while we'd be traveling, I would not be vacationing. (I am, of course, supremely fortunate to live in an age in which I can stay in contact with my studio, and work consistently and diligently, no matter my global position—out of sight, but seldom out of reach.)

As important as the fact of travel is the *way* we do it. I often say that the best possible journey is one that doesn't go entirely as planned. Let's face it: even if you're a nervous traveler, following a perfectly coordinated itinerary that comes off without a hitch is, *enfin*, slightly boring. Excitement derives from the surprise element—the worm of possibility—creeping into the interstitial spaces of one's well-constructed timetable. The best itinerary leaves room for the unexpected, the chance to go off in pursuit of something you've stumbled upon along the way, whether for half an hour or a few days. True, we *think* we're going on an excursion to see X, Y, and Z. In fact, consciously or otherwise, the true objective of every trip (actual, artistic, intellectual, or otherwise) is the lucky accident—that, I believe, is what defines a *journey*.

There is a corollary, to be sure, in what I do, to wit: an overdetermined design is like an itinerary that holds no room for surprise. At the most basic level, that translates into leaving a few blank spots in an interior—otherwise there's no room, or reason, to do any collecting. When a client makes decisions about art, objects, or furnishings, she or he is contributing to, and indeed expanding upon, the story of home. The outcome is a layered experience: layers of time, style, personal history—the moment and everything that lies behind it.

I've never liked eclecticism for its own sake, the idea of slapping a few wildly disparate elements together to achieve a cool, funky vibe. That approach to design I find to be trendy, skin-deep, and possessed of the shortest shelf life imaginable. But a design in which the juxtapositions, however unlikely, grow out of a consistency of vision, a depth of planning and consideration, will always be resonant, and receptive to new ideas and directions. Like a well-conceived journey, a judiciously crafted interior combines a strong spine of intention with an eager willingness to be astonished.

No less challenging is the need to personalize, and that is something else—something essential—that I have learned: more often than not, the great discovery of a voyage is not an unexplored patch of the planet, but rather an undiscovered *individual*. Scott and I have witnessed wonders, we've sailed past erupting volcanoes, sat on the sea floor as vast kaleidoscopic schools of fish whirled overhead, we've stood atop mountains in thin, lucid air and looked out across landscapes of unimaginable beauty—truly, the two of us are blessed. But more than the splendors of ancient Egypt, I remember the skill and modesty of the boat captain who piloted us down the Nile; more than the magnificent 15th-century astronomical clock in Prague's Old Town, I remember the fellow who elaborated upon its workings to us in the warmth of an Art Deco café. When I close my eyes, and conjure up a map of the world, I see, not destinations, but faces; I see friends. That is the ultimate pleasure and purpose of travel—just as the objective of a successful interior design is not the display of wealth, taste, or sophistication, but to make a home for those one loves, whether for reasons of common blood or common purpose.

Not to stretch a point, but designing someone's home is also a voyage—one on which I am very much the tour guide. Potential clients have typically been recommended to me by friends who explained how the process changed their lives: how they went from, in effect, negotiating an uneasy truce with their living situation to having a home that facilitated their needs—not only decoratively and functionally, but in terms of their greater aspirations and longings. That is, in fact, what we aim to do. But rather than telling clients what we think they should have (or want to give them), we first learn their story—and then help them to tell it.

In my experience, individuals tend to fall into one of two categories: there are finders, and then there are seekers. In terms of home design, the finders typically have a "fantasy" house they want to build, the showplace they promised themselves as a reward for all the long days and nights of hard work. The seekers, conversely, are in pursuit of something quite different, a place that can support and encourage personal growth; they want to rediscover their sense of wonder. They've fulfilled that fantasy, and now want to move beyond it, move into a promising unknown to see what awaits. These, I find, are the best kind of clients, at least for me: people who have found, and now wish to seek again—people who say, "Let the journey begin."

When, as a boy, I piloted my single-masted Whaler across Mullet Lake, I fantasized that someday—when I grew up—I'd journey to a place where no man or woman had ever before set foot. Now, half a century later, I've come to terms with the fact that such a place probably no longer exists. There is, in all likelihood, no spot on the planet where I can see what has never before been seen.

But with age comes wisdom (or so they claim), and I understand that being first is ultimately not the point. The point—at least for me—is meaning. I think sometimes about a visit to the Serengeti, when it occurred to me, listening to the roar of lions as I lay in bed one night, that the resplendent Masai tribesmen standing guard outside my tent were there, not for decoration, but for a purpose—that is, to keep us all from being eaten. Had I simply picked up a picture book and admired the tribe's dress and customs then that would have been the limit of my understanding and appreciation. Putting my life in their hands changed everything—indeed, as the poet said, changed it utterly.

I like to think that going the distance has made me a better global citizen. I know it has made me a better designer. And I know, too, that even if I never go where no one else has been, I can still attempt to see everything there is to see with my own eyes, and to understand—and that will be a life well lived.

ON THE VALUE OF FRIENDSHIP

If fair-weather friends are unreliable, does it follow that those met beneath stormy skies are bound to endure? That has proven to be the case in my life: one of the most enriching of friendships was begun, by design, on a rainy day.

James S. Offield—Jim—is the great grandson of William Wrigley Jr., of chewing gum and stadium fame, and knows as much about life, I'd wager, as Franz Liszt, that famously worldly individual. Yet Jim is also blessed with a particularly American charm, curiosity, and courtesy, as I discovered when he first called me, out of the blue, just over 20 years ago. At the time, I'd recently started my business, and was on a visit to my family's cottage in northern Michigan. I picked up the phone, Jim introduced himself, and explained that he'd purchased a cottage of his own nearby, and wished to speak with me about re-doing it. But, he added, he didn't want to disturb my vacation, and said he'd wait for the next inclement day to invite me over to see the place. Amused and intrigued, I agreed.

Sure enough, it wasn't until a furious storm pounded the roof that the phone rang again. I drove over to his club, and, as we lunched, Jim and I discovered that we were cut from similar familial cloth— we were both descended from early 20th-century Midwestern industrialists, and both cottage people, and the connections continued from there. By the end of the meal Jim and I had ceased to be strangers: personal continuity, with remarkable speed, had birthed trust.

This manifested itself after I'd toured his cottage, and offered my thoughts. Jim gave me a completion date about a year hence, told me to seek out whatever resources and subcontractors I required, and suggested I get started right away. For a young designer with a brand new business, it represented an extraordinary opportunity— something other than rain had fallen from the skies.

Other than a single three-hour meeting, I didn't see Jim again until—on the precise day he'd requested—we turned over the keys. Jim demonstrated his satisfaction in the best of ways, by not only engaging us repeatedly in subsequent decades, but by recommending the firm to his mother, brother, and daughter. For Jim and his family, I've completed, as of this writing, 28 projects in 21 years.

Remarkably, that's not the best of it, for once the work on that first cottage was wrapped up, a friendship as beautiful as the one between Rick and Captain Renault in *Casablanca* was launched. I've said that Jim is curious. He is also a sailor, and, learning of my own interest and experience, suggested that we (and eventually our partners) do some exploring together. At that time, I'd done a bit more traveling than had Jim, and he was interested to see what I'd seen, hear what I'd learned, and to create new situations that would enable us to expand our knowledge and enrich our lives. That desire—to build a friendship based on the idea that every moment is precious and none should go to waste—remains to this day one of the greatest gifts I've ever received.

I have benefitted as well from Jim's special ability to successfully pursue personal and professional relationships without letting them get in the way of each other. Though it might not seem so, this is extraordinarily difficult to manage. In any business, the temptation for a client to lean on a friendship is great, but Jim has never once succumbed to it, not even when his extraordinary generosity might have made me susceptible. Jim's integrity—there is no other word for it—has in turn inspired me to show him the same unwavering respect.

That doesn't mean, however, that our travels haven't immeasurably enriched the work we've done together. Jim has often asked me to take him places that have influenced my thinking and tastes, so he can experience first-hand what they mean to me. And because he's possessed of an inexhaustible thirst for understanding, Jim is forever asking me to articulate my feelings, to interpret, explain, even defend. This has made me a better designer in many ways. Jim's insistence that I clearly communicate the nature of an emotion has led me, consciously and otherwise, to apply those articulated ideas to the projects we've created together: you might say that we take joint ownership of them. This is patronage in the very best sense of the word—and again, I am grateful.

Jim is deep-souled, loving, wise, fun—an entirely singular individual in every way. I'm proud to call him my friend, and to have learned so many things from him, uppermost the value— the true value—of friendship. And it is a pleasure to offer, in print, my thanks to a fellow with whom, rain or shine, it's always fair weather.

ACKNOWLEDGEMENTS

One of the more interesting journeys that I have taken has been the creation of this book—a trip that would not have been possible without the vision and guidance of Jill Cohen, who enabled it to all come together. My thanks to Marc Kristal, who helped me to shape the text; to Jorge Gera, whose lovely photos grace nearly every page; and to Irene Chuang in my office, who pulled all the bits and pieces together and kept the project on track.

A very special thanks to the awesome crew at Images Publishing— Paul Latham, Nicole Boehringer, and Gina Tsarouhas—and to Adriano Marcusso, for his beautiful illustrated maps.

For their cogent and thoughtful advice on all things related to this book in particular and my career in general, a most heartfelt thank you to Keith Granet, Meg Touborg, and Erik Perez. I must also acknowledge my amazing travel guru, Peter Carideo, who has gotten me around the world many times, in style and comfort—and rescued me on countless occasions when things went awry.

My gratitude as well to my business partner, John Cialone, and the balance of our management team, including Teresa Stuart and Rick Wetzel, for making it possible for me to do so much, and to have the time to travel widely; and to the entirety of my design team for their creativity and dedication to our craft.

I could not do what I would without my frequent creative collaborators at Rugo/Raff LTD Architects; Neumann Mendro Andrulaitis Architects; and Hoerr Schaudt Landscape Architects. And all of us remain grateful to the builders of the fine homes in these pages: Paul Franz Construction; The I. Grace Company; J.L. LaVallee Construction; Andy Vandermale Construction; Ernie Dollard Construction; Randall Stofft; Tip Top Builders and Delta Marine.

None of what you've seen here would have come to pass without a truly extraordinary collection of clients, notably the ones whose homes appear in these pages: John and Linda Baker; Mark and Cathy Bissell; Fred and Suzie Fehsenfeld; Jim and sujo Offield: and Greg and Stacey Renker.

My deepest gratitude to my family for showing me the way and keeping it real. And last but never least, a very special thank you to my wonderful, kind, adventuresome, and patient husband Scott, with whom I've shared and created this amazing journey over the past 24 years.